Winter Air Quality in Yellowstone National Park
2007 - 2008

Natural Resource Technical Report NPS/NRPC/ARD/NRTR—2008/139.

John D. Ray, Ph.D.
U.S. Department of the Interior
National Park Service
Natural Resource Program Center
Fort Collins, Colorado

November 2008

U.S. Department of the Interior
National Park Service
Natural Resource Program Center
Fort Collins, Colorado

The Natural Resource Publication series addresses natural resource topics that are of interest and applicability to a broad readership in the National Park Service and to others in the management of natural resources, including the scientific community, the public, and the NPS conservation and environmental constituencies. Manuscripts are peer-reviewed to ensure that the information is scientifically credible, technically accurate, appropriately written for the intended audience, and is designed and published in a professional manner.

The Natural Resource Technical Reports series is used to disseminate the peer-reviewed results of scientific studies in the physical, biological, and social sciences for both the advancement of science and the achievement of the National Park Service's mission. The reports provide contributors with a forum for displaying comprehensive data that are often deleted from journals because of page limitations. Current examples of such reports include the results of research that addresses natural resource management issues; natural resource inventory and monitoring activities; resource assessment reports; scientific literature reviews; and peer reviewed proceedings of technical workshops, conferences, or symposia.

Views, statements, findings, conclusions, recommendations and data in this report are solely those of the author(s) and do not necessarily reflect views and policies of the U.S. Department of the Interior, National Park Service. Mention of trade names or commercial products does not constitute endorsement or recommendation for use by the National Park Service.

Printed copies of reports in these series may be produced in a limited quantity and they are only available as long as the supply lasts. This report is also available from the Air Resources Division website (http://www.nature.nps.gov/air/) or the Natural Resource Program website (http://www.nature.nps.gov/publications/NRPM) on the internet, or by sending a request to the address on the back cover.

Please cite this publication as:

Ray, J. D. 2008. Winter air quality in Yellowstone National Park: 2007—2008. Natural Resource Technical Report NPS/NRPC/ARD/NRTR—2008/139. National Park Service, Fort Collins, Colorado.

NPS D-1302, November 2008

Contents

Figures

Tables

Appendixes

Executive Summary

The air quality in Yellowstone National Park was monitored at two locations as part of the adaptive management program on the use of over-snow winter motor vehicles. The leading indicators used were ambient concentrations of carbon monoxide (CO) and particulate matter of 2.5 micrometers or less ($PM_{2.5}$).

The West Entrance near the town of West Yellowstone, MT, is the primary indicator for overall air quality and the relationship to traffic, because detailed entry counts could be obtained at that site. Old Faithful is a destination for most of the winter use vehicles; CO and $PM_{2.5}$ concentrations are lower at Old Faithful than at the West Entrance.

This report is an update to prior air quality and emission studies. The notable findings this year are:

- Maximum hourly concentrations of CO and PM2.5 are up slightly at the West Entrance, but are nearly the same as last year at Old Faithful.

- Air quality at Yellowstone meets the national standards set by the Environmental Protection Agency (EPA) for CO and $PM_{2.5}$ to protect human health. The CO air pollutant, however, is present above natural regional background concentrations (between 0.1 and 0.2 ppm) in areas near vehicle routes, especially during the winter.

- There is a high degree of uncertainty in changes associated with winter traffic at the West Entrance or Old Faithful to any differences in measured air quality during the winter 2007-2008 season. Weather and traffic density are important factors to explain the daily and hourly variations in ambient air pollutant concentrations.

Acknowledgments

We are grateful for Montana Department of Environmental Quality's (MT DEQ) assistance and for allowing us to use data back to 1998 when they started the West Entrance monitoring station. Gary Nelson and Mary Hektner of the Yellowstone staff were instrumental in setting up the stations and assuring that everything continued to function through the isolation of winter.

Introduction

The effects of winter vehicle exhaust, primarily from snowmobiles, on air quality became an issue in the later 1990's at Yellowstone National Park, WY. For the last several years, ambient air quality monitoring has been conducted at two locations in the Park, as part of the adaptive management plan. The plan is to determine the impact on air quality of implementing the 2004 temporary plan and now the 2007 Yellowstone Winter Use Plan (Federal Register 2007, NPS 2007).

This report is an annual update that summarizes the carbon monoxide (CO) and particulate matter of 2.5 micrometers or less ($PM_{2.5}$) monitoring data from winter 2007-2008 and provides a historical perspective of monitoring data at the park. The primary interest is trends in air quality that might reflect on winter use policy and the present conditions as compared to the national standards (EPA 2008) set by the Environmental Protection Agency (EPA).

A guided snowmobile group meets bison on the road, Feb. 2006. Photo: J. Ray.

CO and $PM_{2.5}$ are known health hazards (EPA 2008) for which EPA has set national standards. In the 1990's the volume of winter vehicle traffic had increased to the point where park staff and visitors were complaining about adverse health effects. Concentrations of CO in the entrance shelters and ambient air along the road were found to be high (NPS 2000). Since that time, positive-pressure fresh-air ventilation was added to the entrance kiosks. Also, a series of winter planning processes occurred, resulting in restrictions on snowmobile numbers and implementation of Best Available Technology (BAT) requirements (Federal Register 2007, Ray 2007) The number of snowmobiles entering the park each day has also decreased dramatically. These measures have reduced the CO and $PM_{2.5}$ concentrations at the West Entrance so they no longer are near the national standards (Ray 2007, Ray 2006, Ray 2005).

The latest in these plans, an Environmental Impact Statement (EIS) and Final Rule governing winter use in Yellowstone National Park was issued in 2007 (Federal Register 2007, NPS 2007). Selected tables from the Final Rule with the limitations on snowmobiles and snowcoaches are reproduced in Appendix B. Continued monitoring of the air quality within the park is used as a feedback on policy as part of the adaptive management plan.

Methods

In-park monitoring

Two ambient monitoring locations were used, one at Old Faithful and another at the West Entrance (Figure 1 and Table 1). The Old Faithful monitoring shelter is located at a site to the east of the winter parking area near the temporary visitor center. Instrumentation at the site included a $PM_{2.5}$ monitor (specifically, a Beta Attenuation Monitor), a carbon monoxide (CO) analyzer, wind speed/wind direction sensors, ambient temperature, and a relative humidity sensor. The digital camera shows the parking area next to the temporary visitor center and warming hut (Figures 2 and 3).

Construction on a new west entrance station started in summer of 2007 and continued into the winter months. Only minor changes in winter traffic flow at the West Entrance was expected from the construction activity.

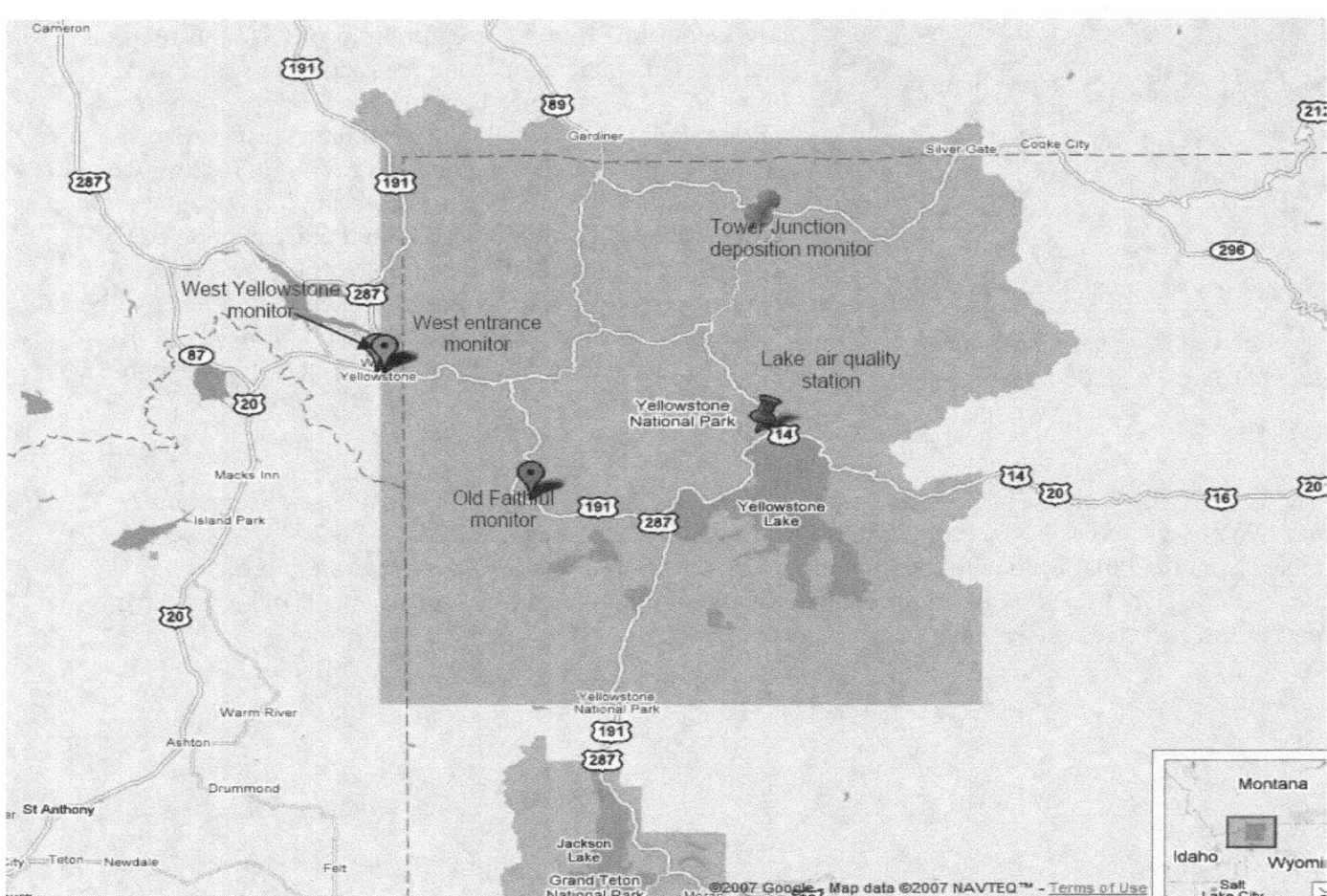

Figure 1. Map with the location of the winter air quality monitors in Yellowstone, in the city of West Yellowstone, and for the two network air quality stations during the winter of 2007-2008.

The NPS field support monitoring contractor, Air Resource Specialists Inc., in cooperation with park staff, operated the station at Old Faithful, processed and validated the data, and provided a data transmittal report. For full details on the monitoring, maps of locations, wind roses, data plots, and data tables, please consult the contractor data reports (Air Resource Specialists, 2007).

The State of Montana collected carbon monoxide, $PM_{2.5}$, and meteorological data at the West Entrance of the park in a cooperative effort. The Montana DEQ shelter is located near the out-bound lane on the northeast side of the west entrance (Figure 4). Data from the West Entrance station were retrieved from EPA Air Quality System (AQS) database and directly from the state of Montana, Department of Environmental Quality (DEQ) (http://www.deq.state.mt.us/AirMonitoring/index.asp). All data collection, validation, and quality assurance steps for the West Entrance data were performed by the state of Montana, DEQ.

West Yellowstone Monitoring

The state of Montana opened a monitoring station in West Yellowstone, MT, starting on January 1, 2007. The location is marked on the aerial view in Figure 4 and site information is in Table 1. Several snowmobile rental businesses and snowcoach departure points are within a three block radius. This city-center monitoring site gives a good indication of the CO and $PM_{2.5}$ concentrations from activities within the resort town.

Other Air Quality Monitoring

Two other air quality monitoring stations are located in the park, one near the Lake maintenance facility and the other near the Tower Junction range office. The Lake station measures ozone, meteorology, sulfate, nitrate, nitric acid, sulfur dioxide, and speciated particulate matter as part of the CASTNet and IMPROVE monitoring networks (http://www.nature.nps.gov/air/monitoring/index.cfm). The station at Tower measures wet deposition for mercury, sulfate, nitrate, and ammonium as part of the NADP/NTN national deposition monitoring network (http://www.nature.nps.gov/air/monitoring/wetmon.cfm). Winter vehicle traffic is very light past these stations and they do not measure CO. Data from these stations can be obtained from links on the Web addresses given above. Neither station provided data used in this report.

Table 1. Monitoring station information for data used in this report.

Site Name	AQS_ID	Latitude	Longitude	Elevation	Parameters
Old Faithful	55-039-1012	44.457	-110.831	2246 m	CO, $PM_{2.5}$, winds, temperature, RH
West Entrance	30-031-0013	44.657	-111.092	2040 m	CO, $PM_{2.5}$, winds, temperature
West Yellowstone	30-031-0016	44.66	-111.10	2041 m	CO, $PM_{2.5}$

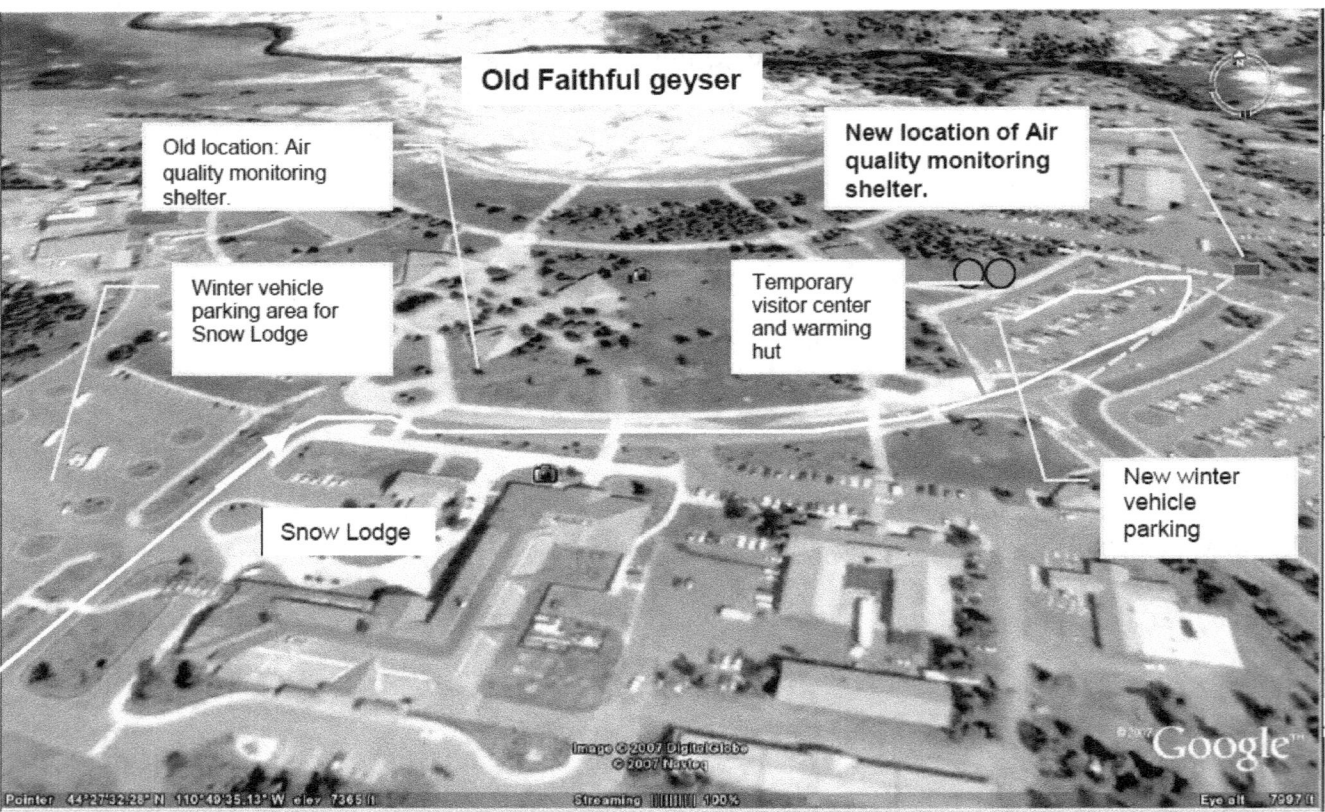

Figure 2. Aerial view of Old Faithful area showing the new locations of the winter vehicle parking and the air quality monitoring station to the east of the old locations. Old Faithful geyser is in the upper background. Red squares are winter vehicle parking areas. The green dashed lines are the approximate view of the monitoring station camera.

Figure 3. Camera view of the parking lot from the new monitoring shelter location at Old Faithful. The cone-shaped roofs of the warming hut and temporary visitor center are seen behind the yellow snowcoaches. http://www.nature.nps.gov/air/webcams/parks/yellcam/yellcam.cfm

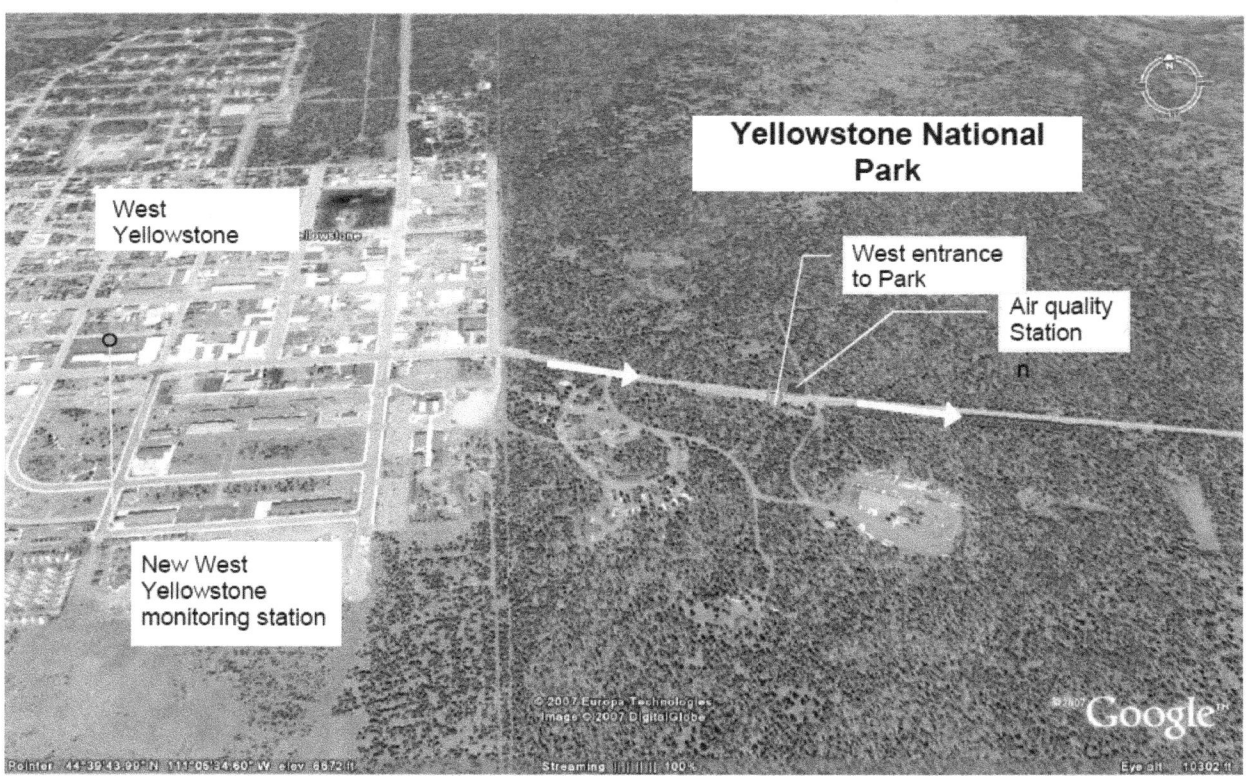

Figure 4. Aerial view of the West Entrance area near the town of West Yellowstone, MT. The air quality monitoring station is on the north side of the road near the roofed entrance structure. Winter vehicles queue up on the west side of the gate. The monitoring station in West Yellowstone city center is marked with a red dot.

Results and Discussion

Summary statistics

The hourly data is summarized here for comparison to the National Ambient Air Quality Standard (NAAQS) set by EPA for CO and $PM_{2.5}$ and to several other statistical metrics used in prior reports. The standards given in Table 2 are for averaging periods of 1-hour, 8-hours, or 24-hours and are normally collected over a year, however, the data summary tables are only for the winter vehicle traffic period in Yellowstone National Park, a three-month period when snow conditions are acceptable.

As can be see from Table 3, the West Entrance station continues to have higher CO concentrations than the Old Faithful station and the concentrations have come down since the winter of 2002-2003. This last winter of 2007-2008 the CO concentrations have increased slightly at the West Entrance and remained about the same at Old Faithful. The maximum 1-hour and 8-hour CO have approximately doubled from winter 2006-2007 to winter 2007-2008 at the West Entrance. This is the first year since monitoring began that the maximum 8-hr average CO concentrations have held steady or increased in Yellowstone during the winter season.

The $PM_{2.5}$ was also up slightly at the West Entrance (Table 4). At the Old Faithful station, the $PM_{2.5}$ is higher than last winter. The new parking area and air quality station location, started in winter 2006-2007, lead to a shift to lower values than previously measured; that pattern continued.

Neither the CO nor the $PM_{2.5}$ at the monitoring stations in Yellowstone are near violating the NAAQS. However, the concentrations are above the regional background (Warneck 1988, Brasseur et al. 1999) for CO which is below 0.2 ppm and the winter CO continues to be higher than the values measured during the summer when visitor and vehicle traffic are high.

Table 2. Ambient air quality standards (AAQS) for carbon monoxide (CO) and particulate matter less than 2.5 micrometers ($PM_{2.5}$). (PPM = Parts Per Million; $\mu g/m^3$ = Micrograms per cubic meter)

Standard	Pollutant	1-hr CO (ppm) [1]	8-hr CO (ppm) [1]
National AAQS	CO	35	9
Montana AAQS	CO	23	9
Wyoming AAQS	CO	35	9

Standard	Pollutant	24-hr $PM_{2.5}$ 98th percentile ($\mu g/m^3$) [2]
New NAAQS [3]	$PM_{2.5}$	35
Montana AAQS	$PM_{2.5}$	35
Wyoming AAQS	$PM_{2.5}$	65

1. Not to be exceeded more than once per year. Link to EPA NAAQS standards http://www.epa.gov/air/criteria.html ; WY DEQ http://deq.state.wy.us/aqd/standards.asp ; MT DEQ http://www.deq.state.mt.us/AirMonitoring/citguide/appendixb.html
2. The 3-year average of the 98th percentile of 24-hour concentrations at each monitor within an area must not exceed 35 $\mu g/m^3$. The winter 98th percentile in the associated tables is given only to demonstrate the improvement between winter seasons. Comparison with the annual standard is not shown. For consistency, the 24-hour day is used to average the hourly $PM_{2.5}$.
3. Revised $PM_{2.5}$ standard by EPA Oct. 2006, down from 65 $\mu g/m^3$.

Table 3   Statistical comparison of CO (ppm) between Yellowstone NP winter monitoring stations.

Old Faithful

Winter CO	2007-2008	2006-2007 [1]	2005-2006	2004-2005	2003-2004	2002-2003
Max 1-hr	**0.9**	0.9	1.6	1.6	2.2	2.9
% of Std	2%	3%	4%	4%	6%	8%
Max 8-hr	**0.4**	0.4	0.5	0.8	0.9	1.2
% of Std	5%	4%	6%	7%	10%	13%
Average	**0.19**	0.27	0.18	0.12	0.26	0.24
90th percentile[2]	**0.24**	0.19	0.26	0.29	0.5	0.5

West Entrance

Winter CO	2007-2008	2006 - 2007	2005-2006	2004-2005	2003-2004	2002-2003
Max 1-hr	**6.1**	3.7	2.1	2.8	6.4	8.6
% of Std	17%	11%	6%	8%	18%	25%
Max 8-hr	**1.6**	0.8	0.9	1.0	1.3	3.3
% of Std	18%	9%	10%	11%	14%	37%
Average	**0.23**	0.19	0.23	0.24	0.26	0.57
90th percentile[2]	**0.4**	0.27	0.40	0.43	0.5	1.3

1   The visitor parking and the monitoring station moved because of construction at Old Faithful.
2   The 90th percentile is not used by the NAAQS. It is a useful measure to track higher concentrations without the points being dominated by possible statistical outliers.

Table 4.   Statistical comparison of PM$_{2.5}$ ($\mu g/m^3$) between Yellowstone NP winter monitoring stations.

Old Faithful

Winter PM$_{2.5}$	2007-2008	2006-2007 [2]	2005-2006	2004-2005	2003-2004	2002-2003
Max 1-hr	**32**	20	56	38	151	200
Max Daily (24-hr)	**8.1**	6.6	9	6	16	37
98th percentile[1]	**5.8**	6.4	9	9	9	21
% of Std	17%	18%	13%	14%	14%	33%
Average	**3.2**	3.3	3.5	4.0	4.9	6.9

West Entrance

Winter PM$_{2.5}$	2007-2008	2006-2007	2005-2006	2004-2005	2003-2004	2002-2003
Max 1-hr	**44**	40	44	21	29	81
Max Daily (24-hr)	**9.5**	8.8	7	6	8	15
98th percentile[1]	**7.8**	8.7	6	6	7	17
% of Std	22%	25%	10%	9%	11%	26%
Average	**2.6**	2.1	1.9	2.9	4.0	8.2

1   Statistic that best relates to the NAAQS standard at the time of the measurement (65 $\mu g/m^3$). Based on daily 24-hr average.
2   The visitor parking and the monitoring station relocated because of construction at Old Faithful.

An air quality monitoring station operated by the state of Montana near the center of the city of West Yellowstone provides a comparison (Table 5). The maximum 1-hr CO is 6.7 ppm compared to the park entrance station value of 6.1 ppm. The 8-hr maximum CO is 2.2 ppm compared to 1.6 ppm. Within the city there are CO emissions from both mobile and small "area sources" that lead to higher CO concentrations over longer periods than those observed in the park. Time series CO concentration plots (Figure 5) show that better than the table statistics. More apparent is the $PM_{2.5}$ concentrations within the city that are 3-4 times higher than at the entrance station. Despite the higher $PM_{2.5}$ concentrations within the city, based on the winter values, the station would not violate the $PM_{2.5}$ NAAQS. Statistical metrics, other than hourly maximum, were all lower for winter 2007-2008 at the city site.

Table 5.   Comparison data from the monitoring station in West Yellowstone city center.

Winter CO	Winter 2007-2008	Jan-Mar 2006-2007 [1]	Units
Max 1-hr	6.7	5	ppm
% of National Std (CO)	19%	14%	- -
Max 8-hr	2.2	2.4	ppm
% of Std (CO)	25%	27%	- -
Average	0.44	0.48	ppm
90th percentile	0.7	0.9	ppm

Winter $PM_{2.5}$	Winter 2007-2008	Jan-Feb 2006-2007 [2]	Units
Max 1-hr	167	119	$\mu g/m^3$
Max Daily (24-hr)	25	32	$\mu g/m^3$
Average	5.6	10.7	$\mu g/m^3$
98th percentile[2]	22	32	$\mu g/m^3$
% of National Std[2]	63%	49%	- -

1   State operated station in West Yellowstone city center started Jan. 1, 2007. AQS ID = 03-031-0016
2   Statistic that best relates to the NAAQS standard. The new standard of 35 $\mu g/m^3$ was used for consistency. Based on daily 24-hr average.

Traffic effects on air quality

Several factors affect the observed air quality at the monitoring stations in Yellowstone. The winter vehicle traffic volume, density, mix of vehicles, and time of day all affect measured pollutant levels most at the West Entrance. In addition, meteorological factors control the amount of mixing and how long the pollutants stay in an area. For example, a shallow surface boundary layer, when the conditions are cold, the sky overcast, and wind speeds low, would contain the vehicle emissions in the air thus leading to higher observed concentrations (Ray 2007, Ray 2006).

As in past years, hourly inflow traffic was counted by the entrance-gate staff according to vehicle type. Vehicle models, vehicle age, or ownership were not identified. A second vehicle counter method was used at the West Entrance based on a radar detector device that could record both entrance and exit counts. The radar detector could also recognize a snowmobile compared to the much larger snowcoach.

At Old Faithful, a less quantative approach was used based on rough counts from digital camera images that were taken every 15 minutes (Air Resource Specialists 2007). This method is imperfect because what is being counted is basically the number of parked and not-operating vehicles within the camera view. What is obtained from the camera image is the approximate timing of activity, some idea of the mix of vehicles, and indications of the weather and snow conditions.

The daily pattern of entry traffic at the West Entrance was very similar in winter 2007-2008 to what has been reported before (Ray 2007, Ray 2006, Ray 2005). Snowmobile traffic was mostly in the morning with a peak in the 9-10 am period. Snowcoach traffic tended to start an hour earlier, peaks in the 9-10 am period then has a secondary peak that occurs at the noon hour. The CO and $PM_{2.5}$ follow the traffic daily pattern (Figure 5 for CO or previous reports (Ray 2007, Ray 2006)), but also show the evening exit traffic and what appears to be local city emissions. In Figure 5 the last two winters are represented and illustrate the differences in observed air quality between West Yellowstone, the West Entrance, and Old Faithful. Old Faithful CO concentrations are lower and have a noon-time peak. For the 2007-2008 winter season the mean CO concentrations for the 9 am peak at the West Entrance are about double what was observed the previous winter. Both the West Entrance and Old Faithful have minimum overnight CO concentrations of approximately 0.17 ppm which is near the regional winter background concentration (Warneck 1988, Brasseur et al.1999). The city center monitoring station has overnight minimum CO concentrations of roughly 0.3 ppm which reflect the presence of area sources and light overnight traffic.

Since the 2004-2005 season when the lowest number of winter vehicles entered the park at the West Entrance, the number of snowmobiles has increased. Official counts (NPS Public Use Statistics 2008) of West Entrance snowmobiles were down slightly for the winter of 2007-2008, however, the number of snowcoaches continued to increase (see Figure 6).

Winter 2006-2007   Winter 2007-2008

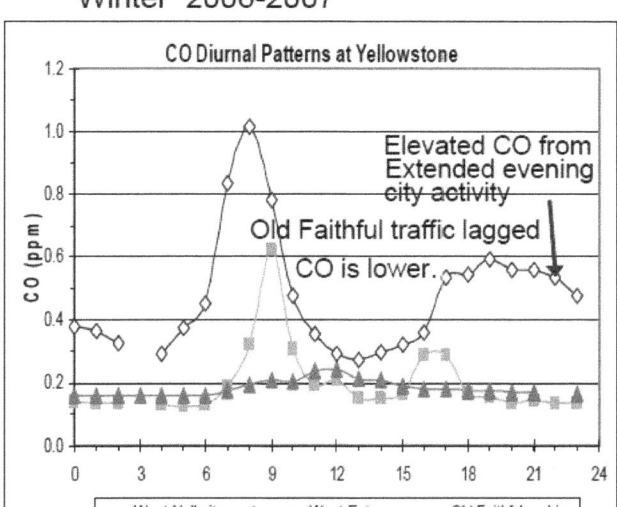 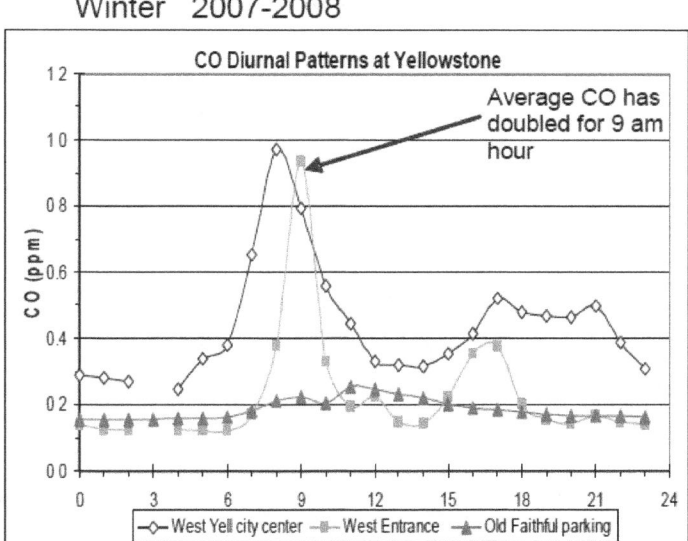

Figure 5.   The daily patterns as mean CO concentrations by hour at 3 monitoring locations reflect the different traffic patterns in the area. The monitors in the park record less CO than the monitor within the town of West Yellowstone.

Neither the mix of traffic nor the total vehicles during the hour of CO measurement were able to entirely explain the few days with the highest hourly CO concentrations. The more general relationships between concentrations and traffic were explored in more detail in a prior report (Ray 2007). There were several important weather factors associated with eight, hourly CO concentrations that were greater than 2 ppm. The factors were: calm winds below 0.2 m/s, cold temperatures less than -25 deg C, and winds from the East. Seven of the eight highest CO concentrations occurred during the 9-10 am period when the traffic is higher.

Construction activities at the new entrance station 550 feet east of the monitor could potentially have influenced the concentrations, however, the timing and pattern of use would be different than the winter vehicle traffic patterns. There was some wheeled-vehicle construction traffic, a front loader, and a propane heater that was used inside the new entrance office. There was no indication in the data of high pollutant concentrations that were out of synchronization with traffic.

Winter traffic volume was related to the observed air quality in previous reports (Ray 2007, Ray 2006). Figures 7 and 8 are updates of charts presented in past reports that show how the air quality improved as the number of snowmobiles entering the park decreased. Second maximum seasonal CO concentrations were up slightly and $PM_{2.5}$ concentrations were about the same based on measurements at the West Entrance in 2007-2008. Overall winter vehicle traffic was down slightly for the season according to the public use statistics (NPS Public Use Statistics 2008). Basically, air quality has stabilized at below 20% of the CO standard in winter over the last 4 years

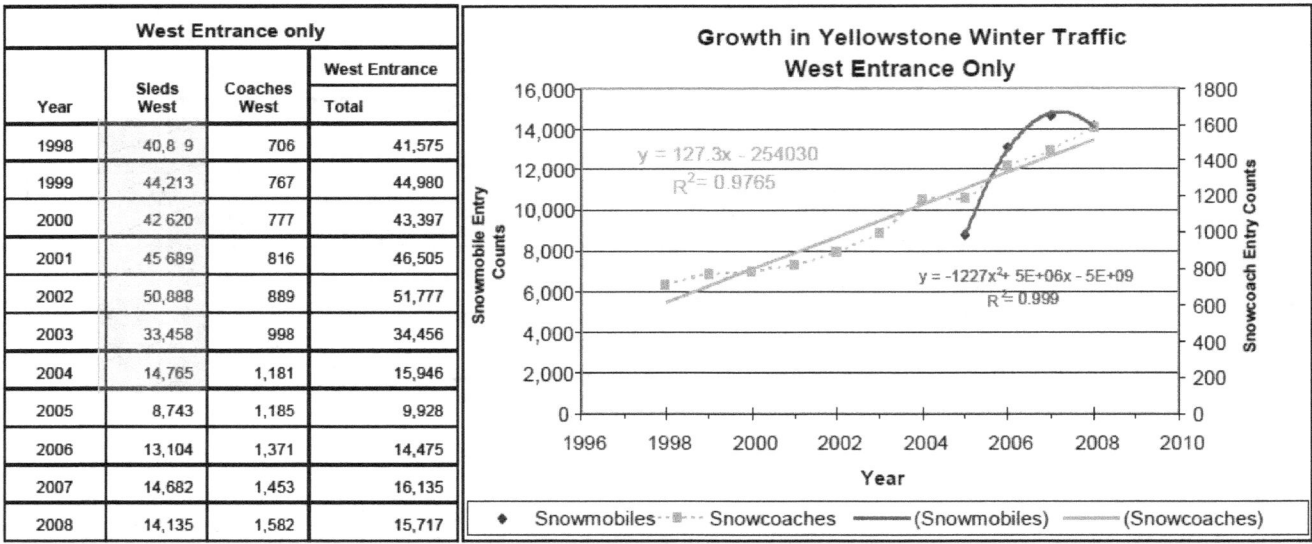

West Entrance only			
Year	Sleds West	Coaches West	West Entrance Total
1998	40,8 9	706	41,575
1999	44,213	767	44,980
2000	42 620	777	43,397
2001	45 689	816	46,505
2002	50,888	889	51,777
2003	33,458	998	34,456
2004	14,765	1,181	15,946
2005	8,743	1,185	9,928
2006	13,104	1,371	14,475
2007	14,682	1,453	16,135
2008	14,135	1,582	15,717

Figure 6. Recent growth in winter vehicle traffic at the West Entrance. Snowcoach traffic has increased every year since 1998. BAT snowmobile traffic was lowest in winter of 2004-2005. Only the 4-stroke BAT snowmobiles traffic volume is shown for the snowmobiles. See figure 7 for traffic pattern prior to 2004.

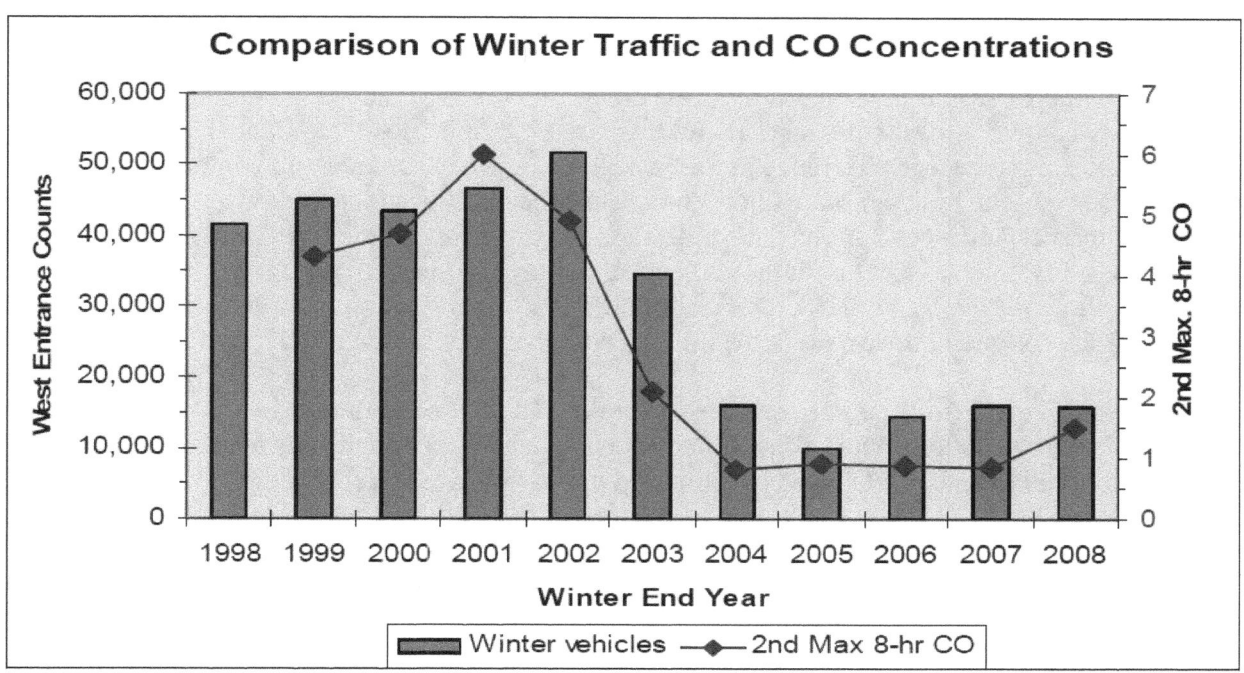

Figure 7. The second highest 8-hour average concentration for the winter season and the amount of traffic through the West Entrance are related. In winter 2003-2004 about 80% of snowmobiles were BAT. Beginning in 2004, all visitor snowmobiles have been BAT certified.

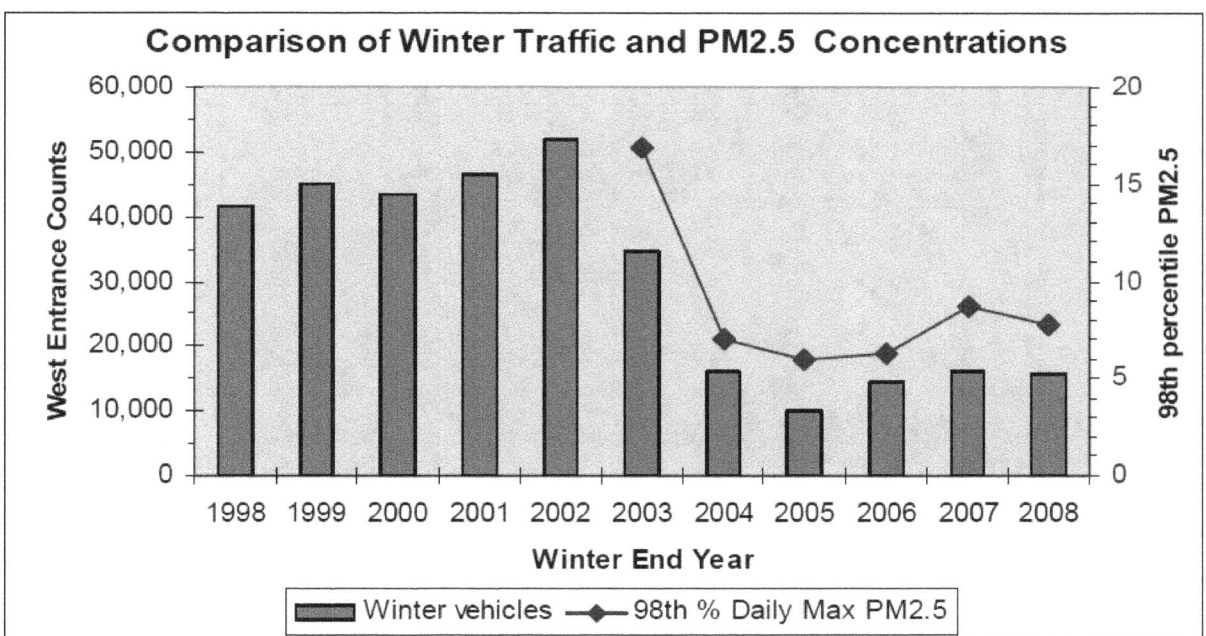

Figure 8. The relationship between the 98th percentile of daily $PM_{2.5}$ and West Entrance traffic counts are compared here by year.

Seasonal Air Quality

The air quality at Yellowstone changes with the seasons in a way that follows the amount and type of mobile sources and the seasonal weather. Changes are most evident at the West Entrance station (Table 6). Summer CO is lower for maximum hourly and maximum 8-hour concentrations than the winter concentrations despite the large difference in traffic volume between summer and winter seasons. The seasonal averages include long periods of night time CO concentrations that are low, so that metric shows little difference at the resolution of the monitoring instruments. During the spring and fall season, when traffic is low or the park is closed, the CO concentration averages go down to the background regional concentrations (Warneck 1988, Brasseur et al.1999). Carbon monoxide air quality is below the standard in all seasons and at its lowest in the fall when the park roads are closed to the public.

The bar charts in Figure 9 illustrate the seasonal differences in CO concentrations. The cyclic pattern is not the natural seasonal pattern. It is a function of the traffic near the monitoring stations. Both maximum hourly and the mean CO concentrations at Old Faithful are lower that the values observed at the West Entrance station. The very large $PM_{2.5}$ concentrations (Table 6) seen in summer and early fall are due to regional wildfire smoke and are not reflected in the observed CO by distinguishable peaks. No trend in the data is evident for the summer season; the number of available seasons of data is still quite small since summer monitoring started only in 2006.

Table 6. Seasonal statistical summary for CO and $PM_{2.5}$ at the West Entrance[1].

Statistics for CO	Winter 05-06	Spring 2006	Summer 2006	Fall 2006	Winter 06-07	Spring 2007	Summer[2] 2007	Fall 2007	Winter 07-08
Max. 1-hr	2.1	0.6	1.3	0.7	3.7	0.9	1.5	1.1	6.1
Max. 8-hr	0.9	0.3	0.9	0.4	0.8	0.3	3.1	0.4	1.6
Season average	0.2	0.1	0.2	0.1	0.2	0.2	0.2	0.1	0.2
90th percentile	0.4	0.2	0.3	0.2	0.4	0.2	0.3	0.2	0.4

Statistics for $PM_{2.5}$	Winter 05-06	Spring 2006	Summer 2006	Fall[3] 2006	Winter 06-07	Spring 2007	Summer[2] 2007	Fall 2007	Winter 07-08
Max. 1-hr	44	15	111	119	40	16	77	25	44
Max. 24-hr	7	4	55	37	9	4	39	11	10
Season average	2	1	6	3	2	2	6	3	3
98th percentile	7	4	31	37	6	4	18	11	8
Period	Dec 15 – Mar 15	Mar 16 – Apr 19	Apr 20 – Oct 31	Nov 1 – Dec. 14	Dec 15 – Mar 15	Mar 16 – Apr 19	Apr 20 – Oct 31	Nov 1 – Dec. 14	Dec 15 – Mar 15

1   CO as ppm; PM2.5 as $\mu g/m^3$

2   Data associated with a wildfire near West Yellowstone occurred overnight on June 28, 2007. CO and PM2.5 high values occurred at the same time. These data were removed from the statistics above as an unusual event.

3   A single outlier hourly value >400 $\mu g/m^3$ was removed from the Fall 2006 dataset.

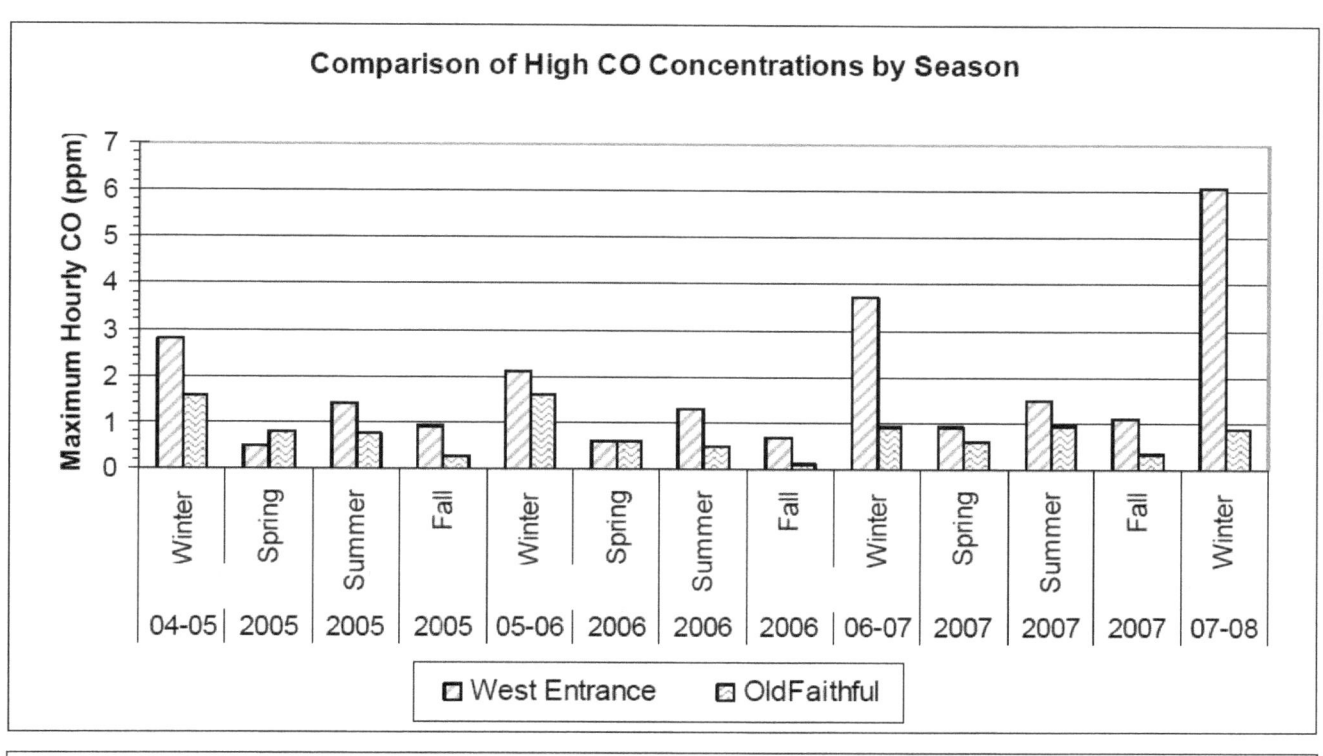

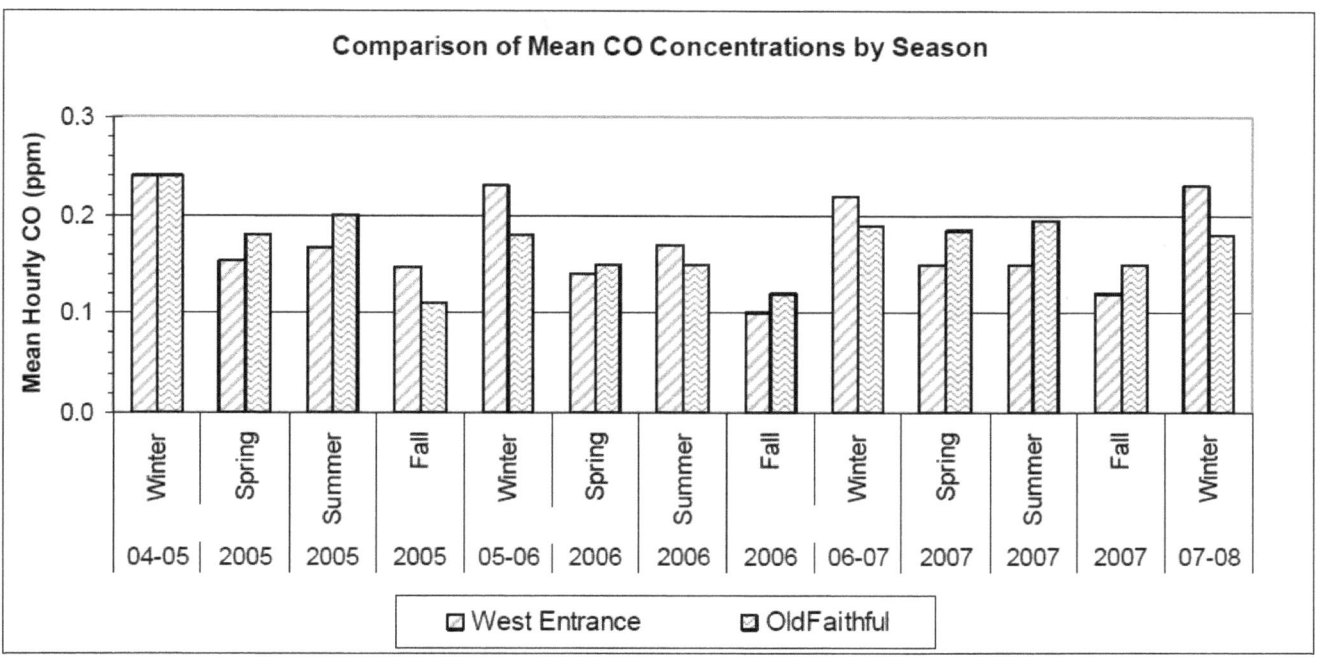

Figure 9. Comparison of maximum hourly (top) and mean hourly CO (bottom) concentrations in different seasons for West Entrance and Old Faithful. Summer concentrations are lower than winter even though there is much more traffic in the summer.

* Data from a June 28-29, 2007 wildfire near West Yellowstone was removed from the summer 2007 statistics.

Conclusion

The air quality has stabilized at the monitoring stations in Yellowstone National Park over the last 4-5 years. This is primarily from the requirement for BAT snowmobiles (NPS 2008) and a much lower number of snowmobiles entering the park. The observed air quality is dependent on several meteorological conditions that dominate changes in the CO concentrations when there are just small changes in the snowmobile traffic. Overall, the current CO and $PM_{2.5}$ air quality is well below the national standards during the winter.

Higher CO and $PM_{2.5}$ concentrations are observed in locations where there is a higher density of vehicles. Total winter vehicles per day or per season are less of a factor than the vehicle density and time of day when they are operating. Early morning operations and high volumes of traffic within the 9-10 am hour contribute to maximum CO and $PM_{2.5}$ concentrations at the entrance stations more so than if the traffic were more spread out.

Entrance gate procedures contribute greatly to the concentration of traffic. That was even more evident in the past when individual entrance passes were sold to winter visitor traffic. Since most snowmobile visits are by guided groups, streamlined entrance pass checking is done that reduces backups at the gate. Other procedures that might be used include assignment of entrance times to the guided groups. This could spread out the traffic so that extremely long lines of snowmobiles didn't develop at the entrance station or along the route into Old Faithful. It would also spread out the traffic at Madison junction so that fewer snowmobiles were there at any one time. This procedure may conflict with soundscape or wildlife interaction management, but might be considered.

Some consideration should be made as to whether the national standards are really the best indicators of good air quality in a natural area such as Yellowstone. At current winter traffic levels the day-time maximum CO continues to be higher than the regional background and higher than the summertime concentrations. This reflects the higher emission rates of the BAT snowmobiles and the older snowcoaches (Bishop et al. 2007) relative to the wheeled vehicles used during the summer, as well as the reduced atmospheric mixing during the winter.

The 2007-2008 winter season had some higher maximum concentrations of CO and $PM_{2.5}$ than seen in the last two winters. Although the difference was small and seemed to be related to weather conditions, and possibly construction activities, the situation should be watched carefully to assure that the winter use plan keeps the air quality at the current conditions or better.

Literature Cited

Air Resource Specials, 2007. Data Transmittal Report for the Yellowstone National Park Winter Use Air Quality Study, 2006-2007. Air Resource Specialists, Ft Collins, CO. Available from http://www.nature.nps.gov/air/studies/yell/yellAQwinter.cfm

Bishop, Gary A., R. Stadtmuller, D. H. Stedman, and John D. Ray, 2007. Portable Emission Measurements of Snowcoaches and Snowmobiles in Yellowstone National Park, University of Denver, Department of Chemistry and Biochemistry, Denver, CO. Online. (www.feat.biochem.du.edu)

Brasseur, G. P, Orlando, J. J., and Tyndall, G. S, 1999, Atmospheric Chemistry and Global Change, Oxford University Press, New York, New York, pages 340-344.

EPA, 2008. CO and PM effects on health. U.S. Environmental Protection Agency, Washington, D.C. Online. (http://www.epa.gov/air/urbanair/6poll.html)

EPA, 2008. National Ambient Air Quality Standards (NAAQS). U.S. Environmental Protection Agency, Washington, D.C. Online. (http://www.epa.gov/ttn/naaqs/)

Federal Register, 2007. Rules and Regulations, Final Rule governing the winter use in three parks. Vol. 72, No. 239 / Thursday, December 13, 2007/ page 70781. Online. (http://www.nps.gov/yell/parkmgmt/upload/finalrule13Dec2007.pdf)

National Park Service, 2007. Winter Use Plans, Final Environmental Impact Statement. U.S. Department of Interior, National Park Service, Washington, D.C. Sept 24, 2007. Online. (http://www.nps.gov/yell/parkmgmt/winterusetechnicaldocuments.htm)

National Park Service, 2008. Snowmobile Best Available Technology (BAT) list for Yellowstone National Park. Online. (http://www.nps.gov/yell/parkmgmt/current_batlist.htm)

National Park Service, Air Quality Division, 2000. *Quality Concerns Related to Snowmobile Usage in National Parks*. U.S. Department of Interior, National Park Service, Washington, D.C Available from: http://www.nature.nps.gov/air/studies/yell/20042005yellWinterSummary.cfm

National Park Service, Public Use Statistics, 2008. Yellowstone visitor and vehicle count statistics. U.S. Department of Interior, National Park Service, Washington, D.C. Online. (http://www.nature.nps.gov/mpur/)

P. Warneck, 1988. Chemistry of the Natural Atmosphere, Academic Press, New York, New York.

Ray, J. D., 2005. *2004-2005 Yellowstone Winter Air Quality Overview Report*, NPS Air Resources Division, Denver, CO. Available from http://www.nature.nps.gov/air/studies/yell/yellAQwinter.cfm

Ray, J. D., 2006. Winter Air Quality in Yellowstone National Park: 2005 – 2006, Air Resources Technical Report NPS/ARD/2007/D-1207. National Park Service, Denver, Colorado. Available from http://www.nature.nps.gov/air/studies/yell/yellAQwinter.cfm

Ray, J. D., 2007. Winter Air Quality in Yellowstone National Park: 2006 – 2007, Air Resources Technical Report NPS/NRPC/ARD/BRTR-2007/065. National Park Service, Ft. Collins, Colorado. Available from http://www.nature.nps.gov/air/studies/yell/yellAQwinter.cfm

Appendix A   Data Access

Air monitoring and emission study reports, journal publications, and data:
http://www.nature.nps.gov/air/studies/yell/yellAQwinter.cfm

Hourly CO, PM2.5, and meteorological data; statistical summary reports:
http://12.45.109.6/

MT DEQ's West Entrance monitoring station data and station information:
http://www.deq.state.mt.us/AirMonitoring/index.asp

Other MT DEQ monitoring stations:
http://svc.mt.gov/deq/QueryAQsitelocation.asp

Old Faithful area webcam, current weather, and current pollutant data:
http://www.nature.nps.gov/air/WebCams/parks/yellcam/yellcam.htm

Appendix B   Selected Material from the Final Winter Use Plan

Materials abstracted from **Federal Register** / Vol. 72, No. 239 / Thursday, December 13, 2007 / Rules and Regulations - Final Rule - Special Regulations, Areas of the National Park System, Yellowstone NP
Amendment to 36 CFR part 7.   Winter Use

This information relates to changes in the Winter Use Plan for 2008-2009 on traffic volumes and emissions. BAT listed snowmobiles are available on the web[13].

TABLE.—DAILY SNOWMOBILE AND SNOWCOACH LIMITS*	Commercially guided snowmobiles	Commercially guided snowcoaches
(i) North Entrance	***20	15
(ii) West Entrance	300	37

** For the winter of 2007–2008 only, the following snowmobile allocations are in effect: West Entrance, 400; South Entrance, 220; East Entrance, 40; North Entrance, 30; and Old Faithful, 30. The following snowcoach allocations will apply in 2007–2008 only: West Entrance, 34; South Entrance, 10; East Entrance, 3; North Entrance, 13; and Old Faithful, 18.

*** Commercially guided snowmobile tours originating at the North Entrance and Old Faithful are currently provided solely by Xanterra Parks and Resorts. Because this concessionaire is the sole provider at both of these areas, this regulation allows the daily entry limits between the North Entrance and Old Faithful to be adjusted as necessary, so long as the total number of snowmobiles between the two entrances does not exceed 40. For example, the concessionaire could operate 20 snowmobiles at Old Faithful and 20 at the North Entrance if visitor demand warranted it. This will allow the concessionaire to respond to changing visitor demand for commercially guided snowmobile tours, thus enhancing visitor service in Yellowstone.

**** These snowmobiles operate on an approximately 1-mile segment of road within the park where the use is incidental to other snowmobiling activities in the Targhee National Forest. These snowmobiles do not need to be guided or meet NPS air and sound emissions requirements.

Snowcoach requirement time lines

Dates	Action
Winter 2008-2009	All snowcoaches operate under a concessions contract.
Winter 2007-2008	Non-historic snowcoaches must meet NPS air emissions – applicable EPA emissions at the time it was manufactured.
Winter 2011-2012	All snowcoaches must meet EPA Tier I emission controls.
Winter 2011-2012	All snowcoaches must meet sound emissions requirement of no greater than 73 dBA.
Winter 2007-2008	Transition allocations on limits to the number of winter vehicles. West Entrance: snowmobiles 400; snowcoaches 34.
2009	Phase-in of EPA Tier II emission standards on multi-passenger gasoline vehicles.
2007	Phase-in of EPA diesel standards.

The park Web site on winter use planning should be consulted for detailed historical changes and the current plans (http://www.nps.gov/yell/planyourvisit/winteruse.htm).

The Department of the Interior protects and manages the nation's natural resources and cultural heritage; provides scientific and other information about those resources; and honors its special responsibilities to American Indians, Alaska Natives, and affiliated Island Communities.

NPS D-1302, November 2008